Chefs' Special

Goan Kitchen

Goan Kitchen

Rita D'Souza

Lustre Press
Roli Books

Acknowledgements

If a soothsayer had told me thirty years ago that I would one day write a cookery book, I would have laughed heartily and asked for my money back! Cooking, which started out as sheer necessity (read drudgery), developed over the years into something of a hobby, and has now become a passion (my children would say obsession).

My husband, Julian, and my children, Kirith, Keya and Kyla, have been at the receiving end of my adventures in the kitchen. Julian has over the past thirty years graciously accepted all my culinary offerings, burnt and otherwise — from rock-hard cutlets to sickly sweet refrigerated cakes — and always pronounced them wonderful! His love, support and enthusiasm for everything I do are life-giving and very humbling.

Kirith (an enthusiastic chef-in-the-making), Keya (whose magic fingers crafted most of the garnishes for the dishes), and Kyla (on whose discerning palate I have come to rely) have been supportive in their unique ways — they have been fearless, frank, even fierce in their criticism, but always lovingly extravagant and exuberant, if somewhat patronising, in their praise!

Cecilia Kerketta has worked tirelessly at my side in the run up to this book and continues to be the backbone of our home. My friend, Sheila Bajaj, nagged me into writing this book and opened the doors to my publishers. And more than anyone else, my mother, Gracie Borges, has always been my idol and inspiration. To all of them, I say: 'Thank you, this book happened because you were there.'

Flavours of Goa

Whoever it was who said about another famous scenic spot, 'If there be a heaven on earth, it is here, it is here, it is here' had obviously never visited Goa — that picture-postcard paradise on the west coast of India. Exotic land and seascape aside, the essence of this Golden Land lies in the *joie de vivre* of its inhabitants, their *sossegado* (relaxed) way of life and warm good-natured hospitality, which can only come from being spoiled by nature's munificence in this Cistern of Plenty: rivers and sea teeming with a variety of fish and shellfish; hillsides lush with vegetation nourished by rich, red soil; and its plains a patchwork of palm-fringed paddy fields.

The traditional cuisine of Goa is the Saraswat cuisine of the Konkan region — a staple diet of rice, fish, vegetable and the ubiquitous coconut that finds its way into every dish, sweet or savoury. Aficionados of Goan food, however, will know that a majority of the fiery, red, vinegary concoctions that popular Goan cuisine has come to be known by, are actually Portuguese in origin. Red chillies and vinegar, the keynotes in any *vindalho*, are both legacies of the Portuguese. The word *vindalho* itself is a derivative of *vinho d'alho* (garlic-flavoured wine vinegar), a Portuguese marinade.

The Portuguese colonised Goa in the early 1500s and embarked on a campaign of religious conversion, that soon led to a cultural, and eventually, culinary conversion. The repertoire of the Goan cook began to include spicy adaptations of relatively bland Portuguese fare, including *chouriço* — the spicy, plump cousin of the Iberian garlic sausage. Some well-loved Goan dishes like *sarapatel* and *cafreal*, travelled to Goa with the Portuguese from their other colonies in Brazil and Africa. As did the chikoo, cashew, tomato, sweet potato, pineapple, pumpkin, and new species of gourds and mangoes. The Portuguese introduced Goans to the culinary arts of baking and confectionery, as well as refined methods of distillation and wine making. These were eagerly absorbed and adapted by the innovative Goan cook, who created a whole new genre of *pãos* and pastries, fruit wines and liqueurs of which cashew and coconut *feni* must reign supreme.

However, rice in all its avatars, and fish remain the backbone of the Goan diet: curried or fried, pickled or dried, at least one of a variety of seafood ranging from the plebeian sardine and mackerel to the majestic kingfish, oysters, prawns, crabs, clams of every size and hue, grace the Goan table at every meal. Tropical fruit like the humble banana and guava, the seasonal mango and jackfruit, or a jaggery-flavoured dessert end the meal on a sweet note.

Special occasions showcase the lobsters, *vindalhos*, *sarapatels*, *xacutis*, *pulaos* and the *pièce de résistance*, *leitão* (stuffed roast suckling pig), followed by a host of calorific sweets presided over by *bebinca*, the queen of Goan desserts. This gourmet feast, punctuated by the strains of a merry *mando* or a soulful *fado*, is washed down with chilled *cerveja* (beer) and Port or home-made wines, with a shot of *feni* to kick-start the proceedings.

Goan cooking, as it has evolved, is fusion cooking in its truest sense: the marrying of diverse flavours, ingredients and culinary techniques, in this case Portuguese and Konkani, to create a unique cuisine that has stood the test of time.

Commonly used Goan Ingredients

1. **Kashmiri chillies**: Goa has a variety of locally grown chillies, but the chilli of choice today is the Kashmiri chilli. The fiery red colour it imparts to a dish disguises its mildness.

2. **Goa vinegar**: Made from coconut palm toddy — used in the cooking of meat, poultry and pork dishes, and as a pickling agent. A milder vinegar has been used in the recipes in this book.

3. **Goa jaggery**: Pyramids or rounds of dark brown or black palm jaggery — used in coconut-based sweets.

4. *Bimblim / Bilimbi*: Sour, gherkin-shaped fruit — used as a souring agent.

5. **Cocum**: A deep red grape-sized berry. The skin is dried and used as a souring agent in fish and vegetable dishes.

6. *Tefla / Teffal*: Dried, acrid, lemon-flavoured berries — used in curries with mackerel and other fish with a high fat content.

7. *Bombil* or Bombay duck is a slim, soft fish, tastes best batter or crumb fried. When dried, it is the perfect monsoon accompaniment to fish curry and rice, when fresh fish is scarce. Fry chopped, dried *bombil* crisp; crumble into a vinaigrette of onions, green chilies, vinegar and salt.

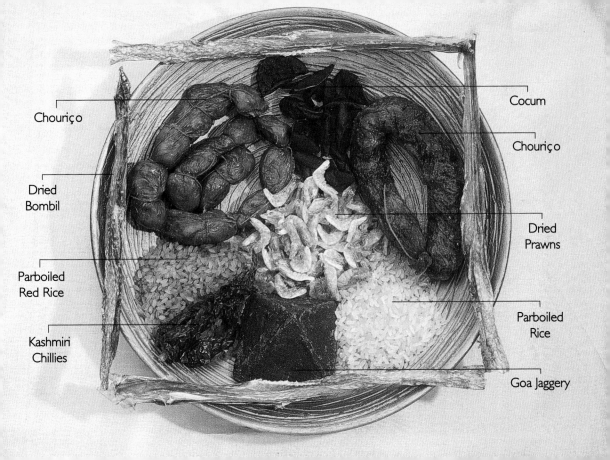

Cocum

Chouriço

Chouriço

Dried
Bombil

Dried
Prawns

Parboiled
Red Rice

Parboiled
Rice

Kashmiri
Chillies

Goa Jaggery

8. **Dried prawns**: Roasted and added to coconut curries and vegetable dishes, relishes and chutneys.

9. **Toddy**: Fresh sap of the coconut palm — used as a raising agent in breads and cakes.

10. *Feni*: Coconut or cashew liqueur, drunk as an aperitif, or used as a preservative in pork dishes.

11. **Goa rice**: Locally grown rice is parboiled before milling and has plump reddish grains with a nutty flavour.

    To cook Goa rice: Boil in plenty of water with salt to taste, on moderate heat, for at least ½ hour. Drain. Cook the rice longer to make *pez* (a rice gruel and Goan comfort food eaten with dried up fish curry or salt fish or pickle)

12. *Chouriço*: There are a number of local versions of the Portuguese garlic sausage. They are stuffed with a spicy filling of cubed pork marinated in spices, vinegar and a dash of *feni*, and sun-dried or smoked over wood fires.

    To cook: Boil whole sausages in water to cover. When cooked, add a few whole pearl onions or thickly sliced onions and cook for a few minutes more. Cut the sausages into 2″ pieces and serve in their own gravy as an accompaniment to *pulaos*.

Basic Preparations

Coconut (*nariyal*) milk: To extract thick coconut milk, soak or grind 1 cup grated coconut in ½ cup warm water. Squeeze out milk and strain.

To extract thin milk, add 1 cup warm water to squeezed out coconut pulp; press through a strainer.

Recheio spice paste: Grind the following ingredients to a smooth paste: 10-12 Kashmiri chillies (*sookhi lal mirch*), ½ tsp cumin (*jeera*) seeds, 12 black peppercorns (*sabut kali mirch*), ½ tsp / 1 gm turmeric (*haldi*) powder, ½ small, onion, chopped (optional), ½" piece ginger (*adrak*), chopped, 12 garlic (*lasan*) cloves, 20 gm tamarind (*imli*), 1 tsp / 3 gm sugar, 1 tsp / 4 gm salt, and 6 tbsp / 90 ml vinegar (*sirka*).

Caldo (chicken / lamb broth): Take 1 kg chicken / lamb bones (with some meat), 2 medium onions, chopped, 1 large tomato, chopped, 5 cups / 1 lt water, 2 tsp / 8 gm salt, a pinch of turmeric (*haldi*) powder, 1" piece ginger (*adrak*), chopped, 1 tbsp / 6 gm coriander (*dhaniya*) seeds, 1" cinnamon (*dalchini*) stick, 4 cloves (*laung*), and 10 black peppercorns (*sabut kali mirch*).

Put the first 6 ingredients into a large pan. Tie the ginger and spices in a muslin cloth and add to the pan. Bring the mixture to the boil, lower heat and simmer for at least 1 hour. Skim off any scum.

Squeeze the muslin bag to extract the flavours. Strain the stock. Remove the meat from the bones and keep aside. Refrigerate stock when cool and skim off any excess congealed fat, if desired.

Add 1 sautéed onion, 1 tomato, cooked meat, and some uncooked pasta / rice for a nutrtious soup.

Camarões Fritos
Fried prawns

Preparation time: 30 min.
Cooking time: 10 min.
Serves: 4

Ingredients:

Prawns, shelled, deveined	1 cup / 200 gm
Kashmiri chilli powder	¾ tsp
Turmeric (*haldi*) powder	¼ tsp
Cumin (*jeera*) powder	¼ tsp
Garlic (*lasan*), minced	¼ tsp / 2 cloves
Ginger (*adrak*), minced	¼ tsp / ¼" piece
Salt to taste	
Vinegar (*sirka*)	1½ tsp / 7 ml
Vegetable oil	4-5 tbsp / 60-75 ml

Method:

1. Mix the prawns with the rest of the ingredients except the oil, and leave to marinate for at least 30 minutes.
2. Heat the oil in a frying pan; shallow fry the prawns, a few at a time, till golden. Remove with a slotted spoon and drain the excess oil on paper towels.
3. Serve hot with wedges of lemon.

Variation: *For a spicier version, marinate the prawns in 3-4 tsp* recheio *spice paste (see p. 11).*

Caranguejos Recheados
Stuffed crabs

Preparation time: 30 min.
Cooking time: 20 min.
Serves: 6

Ingredients:

Crabs, medium, washed	6
Butter	3 tbsp / 60 gm
Onion, large, minced	1
Green chillies, minced	2
Garlic (*lasan*), minced	1 tsp / 6 cloves
Ginger (*adrak*), minced	1 tsp / 1" piece
Turmeric (*haldi*) powder (optional)	¼ tsp
Black pepper (*kali mirch*) powder	a pinch
Salt to taste	
Green coriander (*hara dhaniya*), finely chopped	2 tsp
Lemon (*nimbu*) juice	1-2 tsp / 5-10 ml
Egg, large, beaten	1
Breadcrumbs	¼ cup / 30 gm
Butter	1 tbsp / 20 gm

Method:

1. Plunge the crabs into a pan of boiling water. Boil for a few minutes till they turn red. Drain and cool.
2. Remove the hard shells, wash and keep aside. Carefully remove and discard the stomach pouch and the gills.
3. Lift out as much meat as possible from the body. Crack the claws and remove the meat from within.
4. Heat the butter in a pan; sauté the onion till soft. Add the next 6 ingredients; sauté for 1 minute.
5. Add the crab; cook for 2 minutes. Mix in the green coriander and lemon juice. Remove from heat.
6. Mix in the egg and fill into the crab shells. Sprinkle with breadcrumbs, dot with butter and grill or bake till golden brown on top. Serve hot.

Paparis Recheados
Stuffed poppadums

Preparation time: 25 min.
Cooking time: 10 min.
Serves: 4-6

Ingredients:

Poppadums (*papads*), garlic
flavoured, 5" diameter   10
For the filling:
Vegetable oil   2 tbsp / 30 ml
Onion, medium, chopped   1
Garlic (*lasan*), minced   ½ tsp / 3 cloves
Ginger (*adrak*), minced   ¼ tsp / ¼" piece
Recheio spice paste (see p. 11)   2 tsp / 10 gm
Prawns, shelled, deveined   1 cup / 200 gm
Vinegar (*sirka*)   1½ tsp / 7 ml
Salt to taste

Vegetable oil for deep-frying

Method:

1. **For the filling,** heat the oil in a pan; add the onion and sauté for 2 minutes until soft. Add the garlic and ginger and sauté for 30 seconds.
2. Add the *recheio* spice paste and sauté for a few seconds. Add the prawns and stir-fry till they change colour.
3. Add the vinegar and salt; cook, stirring from time to time, till the prawns are tender and the mixture is almost dry. Keep aside to cool.
4. Dip each poppadum in water and wipe with a clean cloth to make it pliable.
5. Spread a little filling on each poppadum. Roll up firmly. Moisten the edges and pinch to seal.

6. Pour oil in a frying pan to a depth of 1"; fry each stuffed poppadum for a few seconds till crisp. Remove with a slotted spoon and drain the excess oil on paper towels.

7. Cut each poppadum roll into 4 pieces. Pierce each piece with a toothpick. Serve at once.

Variation: *You can also use* balchão de camarão *(see p. 76) as a filling.*

≈

Faster Browning
A pinch of salt will help sautéing onions brown more quickly

≈

Pastéis de Camarão
Prawn puffs

Preparation time: 30 min.
Cooking time: 20 min.
Makes: 25

Ingredients:

For the pastry:

Refined flour (*maida*)	1 cup / 100 gm
Cornflour	½ cup / 50 gm
Salt	1 tsp / 4 gm
Ghee	3 tbsp / 45 gm
Water to bind	

For the filling:

Prawns, shelled, deveined	1 cup / 200 gm
Vegetable oil	3 tbsp / 45 ml
Onions, medium, chopped	2
Ginger (*adrak*), minced	1 tsp / 1" piece
Garlic (*lasan*), minced	1 tsp / 6 cloves
Green chillies, chopped	3
Curry leaves (*kadhi patta*)	4-6
Turmeric (*haldi*) powder	¼ tsp
Black pepper (*kali mirch*) powder	¼ tsp
Green coriander (*hara dhaniya*), chopped	2 tbsp / 8 gm
Vinegar (*sirka*)	2 tsp / 10 ml
Salt to taste	

Vegetable oil for deep-frying

Method:

1. In a bowl, sift together the flour, ¼ cup cornflour and salt to mix well.
2. Rub in 2 tbsp ghee with your fingertips. Add enough water to make a firm dough.
3. Mix the remaining cornflour and ghee into a paste.

4. Roll out the dough into a thin round. Spread the cornflour paste over it, sprinkle a little flour and roll up into a long, thin, tight roll.

5. Cut the roll into 1" pieces. Flatten each piece with your fingers and roll into small discs.

6. **For the filling,** heat the oil in a pan; add the onions and sauté till soft and golden.

7. Add the ginger, garlic, green chillies, and curry leaves; sauté for 1 minute. Add the turmeric powder and black pepper powder; sauté for a few seconds.

8. Add the prawns and stir-fry on high heat for 2-3 minutes. Add the green coriander and salt; continue to stir-fry till the mixture is dry.

9. Add vinegar, adjust seasoning and remove from heat.

10. Spread a little filling on the bottom half of the disc. Fold over to make a half-moon shape. Moisten the edges and press to seal.

11. Heat the oil in a pan; deep-fry the puffs till golden. Remove and drain the excess oil on paper towels.

Note: *Unfried puffs may be frozen for up to 2 months and fried when required.*
Variation: *You can also use a mince filling.*

Pão com Chouriço
Goa sausage rolls

Preparation time: 10 min.
Cooking time: 20 min.
Serves: 8

Ingredients:

Goa sausage meat (*chouriço*)
(see p. 10)   1¼ cups / 200 gm
Onion, large, thickly sliced   1
Vinegar (*sirka*) to taste
Salt to taste
Small loaves of bread   8

Method:

1. Slit the casing of the sausages, and remove the meat. Cook in a pan with 1 cup water for 15 minutes or till the meat is cooked and the mixture is dry. Drain the excess fat.
2. Add the onion and cook for 3 minutes more, stirring occasionally. Adjust seasoning and add vinegar and salt if necessary.
3. Slit the loaves and fill with the sausage meat. Serve at once.

Ameijoas (Tisrio) com Coco

Clams with coconut

Preparation time: 30 min.
Cooking time: 20 min.
Serves: 4

Fish and Seafood

Ingredients:

Clams, medium, washed	4½ cups / 50

Grind to a fine paste with a little water:

Kashmiri chillies (*sookhi lal mirch*)	5
Cumin (*jeera*) seeds	½ tsp / 1 gm
Coriander (*dhaniya*) seeds	¾ tsp / 1½ gm
Black peppercorns (*sabut kali mirch*)	6
Garam masala	½ tsp / 1 gm
Turmeric (*haldi*) powder	½ tsp / 1 gm
Garlic (*lasan*), minced	1 tsp / 6 cloves
Coconut (*nariyal*), grated	1 cup / 75 gm
Vegetable oil	4 tbsp / 60 ml
Onions, medium, finely sliced	3
Salt to taste	
Tamarind (*imli*), soaked in 4 tbsp water	15 gm

Method:

1. Boil the clams in a pan with 1 cup water for 5 minutes till the clams open. Drain. Or prise open with a sharp knife, and discard the empty half.
2. Add the coconut to the ground paste and grind coarsely.
3. Heat the oil in a pan; add the onions and sauté till soft. Add the spice-coconut paste; sauté for 2 minutes. Add the clams, mix well. Add 1 cup water and salt; cook for 10 minutes till done.
4. Mix in the tamarind pulp; cook for 5 minutes more. Adjust seasoning. Cook till the mixture is almost dry
5. Serve hot with rice and curry.

Fofos de Peixe
Fish cakes

Preparation time: 30 min.
Cooking time: 15 min.
Makes: 30 pieces

Ingredients:

Fish, (pomfret / seer / salmon),
 boneless, washed   500 gm
Turmeric (*haldi*) powder   ½ tsp / 1 gm
Potatoes, medium, boiled, mashed   2 / 200 gm
Onions, medium, minced   2
Ginger (*adrak*), minced   1 tsp / 1" piece
Garlic (*lasan*), minced   1 tsp / 6 cloves
Green chillies, minced   2-3
Green coriander (*hara dhaniya*),
 finely chopped   2 tbsp / 8 gm
Lemon (*nimbu*) juice   1½ -2 tbsp / 20-30 ml
Salt to taste
Black pepper (*kali mirch*) powder   ¼ tsp
Eggs, beaten   2

Breadcrumbs / semolina (*suji*)   1 cup approx.
Vegetable oil for shallow frying

Method:

1. Steam the fish with ½ tsp salt, turmeric powder and ½ cup water for 5-7 minutes. Drain and mash well, removing skin and bones if any.
2. Add the remaining ingredients, except the breadcrumbs / semolina and oil. Mix well. Adjust seasoning.
3. On a flat surface, shape small quantities of the mixture into flat round / oval cakes or oblong croquettes. Roll in breadcrumbs / semolina and shallow fry the cakes / croquettes till golden. Serve hot with a spicy tomato sauce.

Peixe Recheado
Fish stuffed with a red spice paste

Preparation time: 20 min.
Cooking time: 20 min.
Serves: 4

Ingredients:

Fish (pomfret / mackerels)	½ kg / 1 medium pomfret / 3-4 mackerels
Salt	¾ tsp / 3 gm
Vinegar (*sirka*) / lemon (*nimbu*) juice	2 tsp / 10 ml
Recheio spice paste (see p. 11)	2-3 tbsp / 30-45 gm
Vegetable oil for shallow frying	

Method:

1. Clean the fish. Remove the internal organs and wash well. Slit the fish on either side of the bone to make 2 deep pockets. Apply salt and vinegar / lemon juice and keep aside for 10 minutes.
2. Stuff the fish with the *recheio* spice paste.
3. Heat the oil in a frying pan; gently lower the fish into the pan, and fry, uncovered, on moderate heat for 5-7 minutes on each side till golden brown. Turn the fish only once.
4. Remove from the pan and drain the excess oil on paper towels.
5. Serve hot.

Variation: *You can also stuff the fish with* chetnim de cilantro *(see p. 74)*

Stuffed Squid: *stuff cleaned squid with the* recheio *spice paste, coat with eggs and breadcrumbs and shallow fry.*

Fish and Seafood

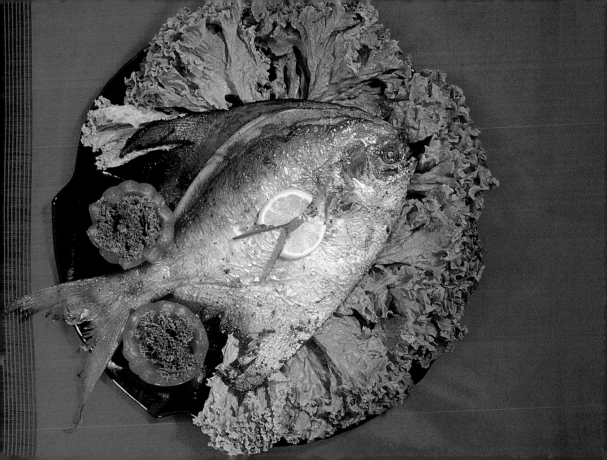

Ambot-Tik
Hot and sour fish curry

Preparation time: 20 min.
Cooking time: 20 min.
Serves: 4

Ingredients:

Fish (preferably shark / catfish),
   washed, cut into 1½" cubes   250 gm
Vegetable oil   3 tbsp / 45 ml
Onion, medium, chopped   1
Garlic (*lasan*), minced   ½ tsp / 3 cloves
Ginger (*adrak*), minced   ½ tsp / ½" piece
Recheio spice paste (see p. 11)   4 tbsp / 60 gm
Salt to taste
Sugar   a pinch
Vinegar (*sirka*) to taste

Method:

1. Sprinkle some salt on the fish and keep aside.
2. Heat the oil in a pan; add the onion and sauté for 3 minutes till soft. Add the garlic and ginger; sauté for 30 seconds.
3. Add the *recheio* spice paste and stir-fry for 2 minutes, adding a little water if necessary.
4. Add 1¼ cups water and bring the mixture to the boil, lower heat, cover and simmer for 10 minutes.
5. Add the fish, salt to taste and sugar. Simmer for 5 minutes until the fish is cooked and the gravy is thick. Adjust seasoning. Add vinegar if necessary. Remove from heat.
6. Serve hot with rice or bread.

Caril de Peixe

Fish in coconut curry

Preparation time: 20 min.
Cooking time: 20 min.
Serves: 4-6

Ingredients:

Fish (pomfret / seer / black pomfret), sliced	250 gm

For the spice paste:

Kashmiri chillies (*sookhi lal mirch*)	8
Coriander (*dhaniya*) seeds	1½ tsp / 3 gm
Cumin (*jeera*) seeds	¾ tsp / 1½ gm
Turmeric (*haldi*) powder	¼ tsp
Coconut (*nariyal*), grated	1¼ cups / 100 gm
Garlic (*lasan*), minced	¾ tsp / 4 cloves
Tamarind (*imli*), walnut-sized ball, cleaned	20 gm
Vegetable oil	2 tbsp / 30 ml
Onion, small, sliced	1
Water	2½ cups / 500 ml
Green chillies, slit	2
Curry leaves (*kadhi patta*)	5-6
Salt to taste	
Sugar	a pinch

Method:

1. Apply ½ tsp salt to the fish. Keep aside for 10 minutes. Wash and pat dry.
2. **For the spice paste**, grind all the ingredients together with ½ cup water to a smooth paste.
3. Heat the oil in a pan; sauté the onion for a few minutes. Add the ground spice paste and sauté for 2-3 minutes.
4. Add the water, green chillies and curry leaves.

Bring the mixture to the boil, lower heat and simmer, partially covered, for 10 minutes.

5. Add salt to taste, the sugar and fish. Cook for 5 minutes, shaking the pan occasionally. Adjust seasoning.

6. Serve hot with steamed rice.

Variations: **Fish curry with cocum**: Add 4-5 pieces of cocum *(see p. 8) while adding the fish. Reduce the quantity of tamarind.*

Prawn and bimblim curry: *Use ½ cup of shelled prawns. Add 5-6 bimblims (see p. 8) to the curry. Omit tamarind.*

Tastier Curries
Add a pinch of sugar to coconut and tomato-based curries to enhance their flavour.

(Photograph on page 4)

Caldinho de Peixe
Fish in a light coconut milk curry

Preparation time: 20 min.
Cooking time: 30 min.
Serves: 4-6

Ingredients:

Fish (pomfret / seer / black pomfret), sliced	500 gm
Coconut (*nariyal*), grated	2 cups / 150 gm
Warm water	1½ cups / 300 ml
Turmeric (*haldi*) powder	½ tsp / 1 gm
Cumin (*jeera*) seeds	1 tsp / 2 gm
Coriander (*dhaniya*) seeds	1 tbsp / 6 gm
Uncooked rice, washed	1 tsp
Garlic (*lasan*), chopped	1 tsp / 6 cloves
Onion, small, chopped	½
Green chillies	1 chopped + 2 slit
Vegetable oil	2 tbsp / 30 ml
Onion, medium, finely sliced	1
Salt to taste	
Sugar	¼ tsp
Vinegar (*sirka*)	1 tbsp / 15 ml

Method 1:

1. Wash the fish, apply 1 tsp salt and keep aside.
2. Grind the coconut with ½ cup warm water, turmeric powder, cumin seeds, coriander seeds, uncooked rice, garlic, onion, and 1 chopped green chilli to extract thick, spicy coconut milk.
3. Grind the coconut again with 1 cup warm water to extract thin, spicy coconut milk. Keep separate.
4. Heat the oil in a pan; add the onion and sauté for 3 minutes till soft.
5. Add the thin coconut milk, salt, and sugar; cook, partially covered for 10 minutes.

6. Add the fish and slit green chillies and cook for 5 minutes till done. Shake the pan to mix. Do not stir.

7. Add the vinegar and thick coconut milk and cook on low heat for 2 minutes, shaking the pan occasionally. Do not let the mixture boil. Adjust seasoning. Remove from heat.

8. Serve hot with steamed rice.

Method 2:

1. Grind the turmeric powder, the next 5 ingredients, and 1 chopped green chilli with a little water to a smooth paste.

2. Extract un-spiced thick and thin coconut milk (see p. 11).

3. Sauté the spice paste after frying the onion.

4. Continue with steps 5-8.

Creamy Coconut Curries
After adding thick coconut milk to a curry do not let it boil, as it will curdle.

Bombil Frito

Fried fresh Bombay duck

Preparation time: 30 min.
Cooking time: 15 min.
Serves: 6

Ingredients:

Bombay ducks (*bombil*) (see p. 8)	1 kg (10-12)
Red chilli powder	2 tsp / 4 gm
Cumin (*jeera*) powder	1 tsp / 1½ gm
Turmeric (*haldi*) powder	½ tsp / 1 gm
Salt	1 tsp / 4 gm
Vinegar (*sirka*)	1½ tbsp / 22 ml
Eggs, beaten	2
Refined flour (*maida*)	½ cup / 50 gm
Breadcrumbs / semolina (*suji*)	1 cup / 120 gm
Vegetable oil for shallow frying	

Method:

1. Remove the head, stomach and intestines of the Bombay duck. Wash well. Remove the bone, by slitting the fish along its length, and carefully cutting around the bone with a sharp knife. Spread the fish open into a flat fillet.

2. Mix together the spices, salt, and vinegar into a paste. Apply the paste to the fish fillets and keep aside to marinate for 15 minutes.

3. Spread the flour on one plate and the breadcrumbs or semolina on another. Roll each fillet in the flour, dip in eggs, and then coat with breadcrumbs or semolina.

4. Heat the oil in a frying pan; gently lower each fillet and fry on each side till golden. Remove and serve with lemon wedges and potato chips.

Caril de Caranguejos
Crab curry

Preparation time: 30 min.
Cooking time: 30 min.
Serves: 6-8

Ingredients:

Crabs, washed	1 kg / 6-8 medium

Grind to a smooth paste with a little water:

Kashmiri chillies (*sookhi lal mirch*)	12
Coriander (*dhaniya*) seeds	1 tbsp / 6 gm
Cumin (*jeera*) seeds	1½ tsp / 3 gm
Black peppercorns (*sabut kali mirch*)	10
Cinnamon (*dalchini*), 1" stick	1
Cloves (*laung*)	6
Garlic (*lasan*), chopped	2 tsp / 12 cloves
Tamarind (*imli*), lemon-sized ball	30 gm
Coconut (*nariyal*), grated	2 cups / 150 gm

Vegetable oil	4 tbsp / 60 ml
Onions, medium, finely sliced	2
Curry leaves (*kadhi patta*)	6-8 leaves
Green chillies, slit	3-4
Salt to taste	

Method:

1. Break the claws and legs of the crabs. Discard the shell, gills, and stomach pouch.
2. Heat the oil in a pan; sauté the onions until soft. Stir in the curry leaves. Add the spice paste and sauté for 3 minutes. Mix in the crab pieces, claws and legs. Add 2 cups water, green chillies and salt. Bring the mixture to the boil, lower heat and simmer, partially covered, for 15 minutes until the crabs are cooked. Adjust seasoning.
3. Serve hot with steamed rice or crusty bread.

Caril de Camarão

Prawn curry

Preparation time: 20 min.
Cooking time: 30 min.
Serves: 4-6

Ingredients:

Prawns, small, shelled, deveined	1 cup / 200 gm
Coconut (*nariyal*), grated	2 cups / 150 gm
Warm water	3 cups / 600 ml
For the spice paste:	
Kashmiri chillies (*sookhi lal mirch*)	8
Coriander (*dhaniya*) seeds	1½ tsp / 3 gm
Cumin (*jeera*) seeds	1 tsp / 2 gm
Uncooked rice, washed	½ tsp
Turmeric (*haldi*) powder	¼ tsp
Garlic (*lasan*), minced	1 tsp / 6 cloves
Vegetable oil	2 tbsp / 30 ml
Onion, small, finely sliced	1
Green chillies, slit	1-2
Curry leaves (*kadhi patta*)	5
Tamarind (*imli*), walnut-sized ball, soaked in ¼ cup water for 5 minutes	20 gm
Sugar	½ tsp / 1½ gm
Salt to taste	

Method:

1. Grind the coconut with ½ cup warm water and extract thick coconut milk. Reserve. Add 2½ cups warm water to the coconut, grind again and extract thin coconut milk. Keep aside.

2. **For the spice paste**, grind all the ingredients mentioned with a little water to a smooth paste.

3. Heat the oil in a pan; sauté the onion for 3 minutes. Add the spice paste; sauté for 1 minute more. Add

the thin coconut milk, green chillies, and curry leaves. Cook on medium heat, partially covered, for 10 minutes.

4. Strain the tamarind pulp and add to the curry with the prawns. Cook for 5 minutes. Add the sugar and salt to taste.

5. Finally, add the thick coconut milk. Simmer without boiling for 2 minutes and remove from heat.

6. Serve with steamed white rice and fried fish.

Variation 1: *Add 10 okra* (bhindi) *cut into 1½" pieces. Omit uncooked rice in the spice paste.*

Variation 2: *Add 1 peeled, sliced mango (unripe) or a few sliced* bimblims *(see p. 8). Omit the tamarind.*

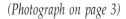

For Soft Flesh
Add hot water to cook meat after browning or it will toughen.

(Photograph on page 3)

Costeletas / Bifes Empanados

Crumb fried lamb chops / steaks

Preparation time: 2 hrs. 20 min.
Cooking time: 30 min.
Serves: 4

L a m b / B e e f

I n g r e d i e n t s :

Lamb chops /
  beef or veal fillet   ½ kg / 8 chops / 15 slices

For the spice paste:

Green coriander (*hara dhaniya*)	1 cup / 60 gm
Green chillies	2-3
Garlic (*lasan*), minced	1 tsp / 6 cloves
Ginger (*adrak*), minced	1 tsp / 1" piece
Cumin (*jeera*) seeds	1 tsp / 2 gm
Lemon (*nimbu*) juice	1½ tbsp / 22 ml
Salt	1½ tsp / 6 gm
Black pepper (*kali mirch*) powder	¼ tsp

Vegetable oil for shallow frying
Refined flour (*maida*)   ½ cup / 50 gm

Eggs, beaten	2
Breadcrumbs	1 cup approx.

M e t h o d :

1. Beat the chops / slices with a rolling pin or meat mallet to tenderise.
2. **For the spice paste**, grind all the ingredients into a smooth paste. Apply the paste to the chops / slices and marinate for at least 2 hours.
3. Heat the oil in a frying pan. Roll the chops / slices in the flour, then dip in beaten eggs. Coat with breadcrumbs and fry for 5-7 minutes on each side till golden.
4. Serve hot, accompanied by a green salad or sautéed boiled potatoes.

Rissoís de Batata e Carne Picada

Lamb / beef mince rissoles

Preparation time: 20 min.
Cooking time: 45 min.
Serves: 6-8

Lamb/Beef

Ingredients:

Lamb / beef mince	500 gm
Vegetable oil	4 tbsp / 60 ml + for frying
Onions, medium, chopped	3
Ginger (*adrak*), minced	3 tsp / 3" piece
Garlic (*lasan*), minced	2 tsp / 12 cloves
Tomato, large, chopped	1
Green chillies, minced	3
Green coriander (*hara dhaniya*), chopped	3 tbsp / 12 gm
Cumin (*jeera*) powder	1 tsp / 1½ gm
Red chilli powder	1 tsp / 2 gm
Black pepper (*kali mirch*) powder	½ tsp
Salt	1 tsp / 4 gm
Vinegar (*sirka*)	2 tbsp / 30 ml
Potatoes, medium, boiled, mashed	6 / 750 gm
Eggs, beaten	2
Breadcrumbs	1 cup approx.

Method:

1. Heat the oil in a pan; sauté the onion till golden. Add the ginger and garlic; sauté for 1 minute.
2. Add the mince; fry on high heat for 5 minutes. Add the tomato and the next 6 ingredients; stir-fry. Add 1 cup hot water, bring to the boil, lower heat, and simmer covered for 10-15 minutes till done. Add vinegar and cook, uncovered, till dry.
3. Take 2" diameter balls of mashed potato seasoned with salt, hollow out and stuff with a little mince. Pinch together to seal. Pat into rounds, dip in egg, roll in breadcrumbs and shallow-fry till golden.

Caril de Almondegas de Carne

Meat ball curry

Preparation time: 30 min.
Cooking time: 30 min.
Serves: 6-8

Ingredients:

Lamb / beef mince	500 gm
For the spice paste:	
Kashmiri chillies (*sookhi lal mirch*)	8
Coriander (*dhaniya*) seeds	2 tsp / 4 gm
Cumin (*jeera*) seeds	½ tsp / 1 gm
Black peppercorns (*sabut kali mirch*)	6
Poppy seeds (*khuskhus*)	½ tsp
Cloves (*laung*)	5
Cinnamon (*dalchini*), 1" sticks	2
Turmeric (*haldi*) powder	½ tsp / 1 gm
Garlic (*lasan*), minced	1½ tsp / 9 cloves
Ginger (*adrak*), chopped	1 tsp / 1" piece
Coconut (*nariyal*), grated	1¼ cups / 100 gm
Bengal gram flour (*besan*)	1 tbsp / 10 gm
or Bread, crumbled	2 slices
Green coriander (*hara dhaniya*), chopped	3 tbsp / 12 gm
Vegetable oil	3 tbsp / 45 ml
Onion, medium, finely sliced	1
Curry leaves (*kadhi patta*)	6-8
Tomato, large, chopped	1
Salt	1½ tsp / to taste
Vinegar (*sirka*)	2 tbsp / 30 ml

Method:

1. **For the spice paste**, grind the ingredients with a little water to a smooth paste.
2. Grind the minced meat with 3 tbsp of the spice paste till smooth. Add the Bengal gram flour or crumbled slices of bread, green coriander and ½ tsp

salt; mix well. Divide the mixture into small balls about 1" in diameter. Keep aside.

3. Heat the oil in a large pan; sauté the onion till soft and golden brown. Add the curry leaves and the remaining spice paste; stir-fry for a few minutes. Add the tomato and sauté for a few minutes until soft and mushy and the oil begins to separate.

4. Add 2 cups water and bring the mixture to the boil. Simmer for 15 minutes.

5. Drop the meat balls in carefully, one by one, and cook gently for 10 minutes or until just cooked. Shake the pan gently from time to time. Do not stir or the meat balls may break.

6. Add the vinegar and cook for 2 minutes. Adjust seasoning. Remove from heat.

7. Serve with *arroz com coco* (see p. 66).

Truely Goan
The key to authentic Goan cooking is to use freshly ground whole spices.

Sarapatel

Diced pork and liver in a spicy curry

Preparation time: 45 min.
Cooking time: I hr.
Serves: 6-8

Pork

Ingredients:

Pork, with some fat, washed, cut into large pieces	1 kg
Pork liver, washed, cut into large pieces	250 gm
Vegetable oil	¾ cup / 150 ml

For the spice paste:

Kashmiri chillies (*sookhi lal mirch*)	15-20
Black peppercorns (*sabut kali mirch*)	15
Cumin (*jeera*) seeds	1 tsp / 2 gm
Cinnamon (*dalchini*), 1" sticks	2
Cloves (*laung*)	7
Turmeric (*haldi*) powder	½ tsp / 1 gm
Garlic (*lasan*), minced	4 tsp / 24 cloves
Ginger (*adrak*), minced	3 tsp / 3" piece
Vinegar (*sirka*)	11 tbsp / 165 ml
Onions, medium, chopped	4
Salt	2½ tsp / 10 gm
Green chillies, slit (optional)	2-3

Method:

1. Boil the pork and liver, separately, in water to cover, for 20 minutes. Keep aside to cool. Lift the pieces of meat out of the stock. Strain and reserve the stock.

2. Cut the pork and liver into small cubes. Separate the cubes into 4 portions and fry each portion in a frying pan with 1 tbsp of oil each time until lightly browned. Keep aside.

3. **For the spice paste**, grind the spices, half the

quantity of garlic and ginger with 8 tbsp vinegar to a smooth paste.

4. Heat the remaining oil in a large pan; add the onions and sauté until soft and golden brown. Add the remaining garlic and ginger; sauté for 1 minute.

5. Add the spice paste and sauté for 3-5 minutes, stirring continuously.

6. Add the fried pork, liver, and salt; mix well. Add 2 cups of hot stock and bring the mixture to the boil. Lower heat and simmer covered, for 30 minutes, till the pork is tender.

7. Add the remaining vinegar, green chillies, and more stock, if necessary; simmer for 5-10 minutes. Remove from heat.

8. Serve hot with *sanna* (see p. 71).

Note: *Cook this dish at least 2 days before serving for the flavours to mature.*

A Dash of Vinegar
The flavour of dishes cooked in vinegar matters and improves on keeping.

Vindalho de Carne de Porco

Pork curry flavoured with garlic and vinegar

Preparation time: 12½ hrs.
Cooking time: 1½ hrs.
Serves: 6

Ingredients:

Pork with some fat, cut into 2" cubes   1 kg
Grind to a smooth paste with 5 tbsp vinegar:
Kashmiri chillies (*sookhi lal mirch*)   15-20
Cumin (*jeera*) seeds   1 tsp / 2 gm
Black peppercorns (*sabut kali mirch*)   ½ tsp
Mustard seeds (*rai*), (optional)   ½ tsp / 1 gm
Cinnamon (*dalchini*), 1" stick (optional)   1
Cloves (*laung*), (optional)   6
Turmeric (*haldi*) powder   ½ tsp / 1 gm
Ginger (*adrak*), minced   2 tsp / 2" piece
Garlic (*lasan*), minced   3 tsp / 16-18 cloves
Salt   2 tsp / 8 gm

(Photograph on page 2)

Vegetable oil	4 tbsp / 60 ml
Onions, medium, finely sliced	4
Green chillies, slit	2
Vinegar (*sirka*)	4 tbsp / 60 ml

Method:

1. Marinate the pork in the spice paste for at least 12 hours in the refrigerator.
2. Heat the oil in a pan; sauté the onions till golden. Add the marinated pork; sauté on high heat for 7 minutes. Add 2½ cups hot water; simmer till pork is tender. Add the green chillies, vinegar, and more salt if necessary. Simmer till the gravy is thick.
3. Cook this dish at least 24 hours before serving with crusty bread or rice.

Galinha Cafreal
Spicy fried / grilled chicken

Preparation time: 4¼ hrs.
Cooking time: 30 min.
Serves: 4

C h i c k e n

Ingredients:

Chicken, legs and thighs	1 kg / 8-10 pieces
Grind to a smooth paste:	
Onion, medium, chopped	1
Ginger (*adrak*), minced	1½ tsp / 1½" piece
Garlic (*lasan*), minced	1½ tsp / 9 cloves
Green chillies, minced	3-4
Green coriander (*hara dhaniya*), chopped	½ cup / 7½ gm
Black pepper (*kali mirch*) powder	¼ tsp
Cumin (*jeera*) seeds, powdered	½ tsp / 1 gm
Garam masala	1 tsp / 2 gm
Salt	2 tsp / 8 gm
Lemon (*nimbu*) juice	3 tbsp / 45 ml
Vegetable oil	4 tbsp / 60 ml

Method:

1. Prick the chicken pieces with a fork.
2. Marinate the chicken in the ground spice paste for at least 4 hours.
3. Heat the oil in a frying pan; sauté the chicken on high heat for 5 minutes, turning once. Lower heat, and cook covered till tender.
4. Retain some gravy, or if preferred, uncover the pan and fry the chicken until brown. Serve with grilled potatoes and tomatoes.
5. Alternatively, brush the marinated chicken with a little oil and grill or cook in a hot oven (200°C / 400°F) till tender and brown.
6. Serve with lemon wedges and a crisp salad.

Xacuti de Galinha
Chicken curry with roasted spices

Preparation time: 30 min.
Cooking time: 45 min.
Serves: 6

Ingredients:

Chicken, cut into 12 pieces	1 kg
Coconut (*nariyal*), grated	2 cups / 150 gm
Onions, medium, sliced	2
Kashmiri chillies (*sookhi lal mirch*)	10
Cumin (*jeera*) seeds	1 tsp / 2 gm
Coriander (*dhaniya*) seeds	1½ tbsp / 9 gm
Poppy seeds (*khuskhus*)	2 tsp / 4 gm
Black peppercorns (*sabut kali mirch*)	6
Cinnamon (*dalchini*), 1" sticks	2
Cloves (*laung*)	8
Star anise (*sakhar phool*)	1
Fennel (*moti saunf*)	2 tsp / 4 gm
Turmeric (*haldi*) powder	½ tsp / 1 gm
Vegetable oil	5 tbsp / 75 ml
Onions, medium, finely sliced	2
Ginger (*adrak*), minced	1½ tsp / 1½" piece
Garlic (*lasan*), minced	1½ tsp / 9 cloves
Salt	2 tsp / 8 gm
Lemon (*nimbu*) juice	2-3 tbsp / 30-45 ml

Method:

1. Grind 1 cup coconut with ½ cup warm water and extract ¾ cup thick coconut milk. Add 1 cup warm water to the coconut again and extract 1 cup thin coconut milk. Keep both aside.
2. Heat a frying pan and dry roast 1 cup coconut till light brown. Dry roast the onions for a few minutes.
3. In the same pan, add 1 tsp oil and sauté the Kashmiri chillies for 1 minute. Remove. Sauté each

of the next 8 ingredients separately with a few drops of oil for a few seconds. Do not allow any of the spices to burn as they will turn bitter.

4. Grind the roasted coconut, onions and spices with the turmeric powder and a little water to a smooth paste.

5. Heat the oil in a large pan; add the onions and sauté till soft and golden. Add the ginger and garlic; sauté for 1 minute.

6. Add the chicken and sauté for 2-3 minutes on high heat till brown. Add the roasted coconut spice paste and mix well.

7. Add the thin coconut milk and salt, mix well, bring to the boil, lower heat and simmer partially covered for 20 minutes until the chicken is cooked and the gravy is thick.

8. Add the thick coconut milk and lemon juice and simmer for 5 minutes. Adjust seasoning.

9. Serve hot with rice or *pulao*.

Note: *For a less rich dish, replace coconut milk with water.*

Baffado de Galinha

Chicken in coconut gravy

Preparation time: 30 min.
Cooking time: 35 min.
Serves: 4-6

Ingredients:

Chicken, cut into 10-12 pieces	1 kg
Coconut (*nariyal*), grated	3 cups / 250 gm

Grind to a smooth paste with a little water:

Kashmiri chillies (*sookhi lal mirch*)	8
Coriander (*dhaniya*) seeds	1 tsp / 2 gm
Cumin (*jeera*) seeds	¾ tsp
Black peppercorns (*sabut kali mirch*)	10
Cinnamon (*dalchini*), 1″ stick	1
Cloves (*laung*)	4
Uncooked rice (optional)	½ tsp
Turmeric (*haldi*) powder	½ tsp / 1 gm
Garlic (*lasan*), minced	1½ tsp / 9 cloves
Ginger (*adrak*), minced	1 tsp / 1″ piece
Vegetable oil	4 tbsp / 60 ml
Onions, medium, finely sliced	2
Green chillies, slit	2-3
Salt	2 tsp / 8 gm
Vinegar (*sirka*)	3 tbsp / 45 ml

Method:

1. Extract 1 cup thick and 1½ cups thin coconut milk from the grated coconut (see p.11). Keep aside.
2. Heat the oil in a pan; sauté the onions till golden. Add the ground paste and fry for 2 minutes. Add the chicken and fry on high heat for 3 minutes.
3. Add the thin coconut milk, green chillies and salt; bring to the boil, lower heat and simmer, partially covered, till the chicken is tender. Add the vinegar and thick coconut milk; simmer uncovered for 5 minutes. Remove and serve with rice.

Beringelas Picantes
Spicy aubergine

Preparation time: 15 min.
Cooking time: 20 min.
Serves: 4-6

Vegetarian

Ingredients:

Aubergine (*baingan*), large, seedless 1 / 400 gm
Grind to a smooth paste with 5 tbsp vinegar:
Kashmiri chillies (*sookhi lal mirch*)   6
Mustard seeds (*rai*)   ½ tsp / 1 gm
Cumin (*jeera*) seeds   ½ tsp / 1 gm
Turmeric (*haldi*) powder   ¼ tsp
Garlic (*lasan*), minced   1 tsp / 6 cloves
Ginger (*adrak*), minced   2 tsp / 2" piece

Vegetable oil   3 tbsp / 45 ml
Garlic (*lasan*), chopped   1 tsp / 6 cloves
Green chillies, chopped   1-2
Granulated sugar   2 tsp / 6 gm
Salt   1½ tsp / 6 gm
Vinegar (*sirka*)   4 tbsp / 60 ml

Method:

1. Wash the aubergine and wipe dry. Chop into 1½" cubes. Do not soak in water or wash after cutting.
2. Heat the oil in a pan; sauté the garlic and green chillies for 30 seconds. Add the ground spice paste and sauté for 2 minutes.
3. Add the aubergine and mix well. Add the sugar, salt, and vinegar. Stir well. Cover the pan with a deep metal lid. Pour a little water on the lid and cook on low heat till soft. Taste and adjust seasoning. Remove from heat.
4. Serve hot as an accompaniment to rice and curry.

Note: *Tastes better the next day.*

Fugad de Repolho
Steamed cabbage

Preparation time: 10 min.
Cooking time: 15 min.
Serves: 4-6

V
e
g
e
t
a
r
i
a
n

Ingredients:

Cabbage (*bandh gobi*),
  finely shredded   400 gm
Vegetable oil   1 tbsp / 15 ml
Onion, medium, sliced   1
Garlic (*lasan*), minced (optional) ½ tsp / 3 cloves
Green chilli, minced   1
Salt   ½ tsp / 2 gm
Coconut (*nariyal*), grated   3 tbsp / 12 gm

Method:

1. Heat the oil in a pan; add the onion and garlic, if using, and sauté for 3 minutes till soft.
2. Add the cabbage, green chilli, and salt. Mix well. Cover with a deep metal lid. Pour some water on the lid and cook the cabbage in its own juices for 10 minutes till soft, but not mushy.
3. Add the coconut and mix well. Serve hot.

Note: *This is the most common method of cooking vegetables, especially gherkins, spinach, red amaranth, red pumpkin, snake gourd, and bottle gourd. Increase the quantity of onions when cooking leafy vegetables.*

Quiabos com Cebolas
Okra with onion

Preparation time: 10 min.
Cooking time: 15 min.
Serves: 4-6

V
e
g
e
t
a
r
i
a
n

Ingredients:

Okra (*bhindi*), washed	500 kg
Vegetable oil	3 tbsp / 45 ml
Onion, medium, chopped	1
Garlic (*lasan*), minced	½ tsp / 3 cloves
Ginger (*adrak*), minced	½ tsp / ½" piece
Turmeric (*haldi*) powder	¼ tsp
Green chillies, chopped	1-2
Vinegar (*sirka*)	1 tbsp / 15 ml
Salt to taste	

Method:

1. Wipe the okra with a cloth. Cut off the tops and discard. Chop into 1" pieces.
2. Heat the oil in a pan; sauté the onion for 2 minutes till transparent. Add the garlic and ginger; sauté for 30 seconds.
3. Add the okra, turmeric powder, green chillies, vinegar, and salt; mix well. Cook covered on low heat till the vegetable is tender. Open the lid and stir-fry to dry up any liquid. Adjust seasoning.
4. Serve hot.

Variations: *Any vegetable can be cooked this way. Omit the vinegar and add tamarind pulp or 1 large tomato instead.*

Melgor / Alsande
Black-eyed bean curry

Preparation time: 20 min.
Cooking time: 30 min.
Serves: 6

Ingredients:

Black-eyed beans (*lobia*),
   soaked for 30 minutes   1¼ cups / 200 gm

For the spice paste:
Kashmiri chillies (*sookhi lal mirch*)   8
Coriander (*dhaniya*) seeds   1½ tsp / 3 gm
Cumin (*jeera*) seeds   1 tsp / 2 gm
Turmeric (*haldi*) powder   ½ tsp / 1 gm
Coconut (*nariyal*), grated   1¼ cups / 100 gm
Garlic (*lasan*), minced   1 tsp / 6 cloves
Tamarind (*imli*), lemon-sized ball   20 gm

Vegetable oil   3 tbsp / 45 ml
Onion, medium, sliced   1
Curry leaves (*kadhi patta*)   6-8
Green chillies, slit   3

Salt   2 tsp / 8 gm
Sugar   a pinch

Method:

1. Boil the beans in water to cover till just cooked. Keep aside.
2. **For the spice paste**, grind the ingredients with ½ cup water to a smooth paste.
3. Heat the oil in a pan; add the onion and sauté till soft. Add the spice paste and curry leaves; sauté for 2 minutes. Add the boiled beans, green chillies, salt, sugar, and 1½ cups water; cook for 10 minutes on moderate heat. Adjust seasoning.
4. Serve hot with steamed rice.

Xengo Temperado
Curried drumsticks

Preparation time: 20 min.
Cooking time: 20 min.
Serves: 4-6

Ingredients:

Drumsticks (*saijan ki phalli*),
cut into 2½" pieces   8

Grind to a smooth paste with a little water:

Coconut (*nariyal*), grated	⅔ cup / 50 gm
Green chillies	3
Cumin (*jeera*) seeds	½ tsp / 1 gm
Turmeric (*haldi*) powder	¼ tsp
Garlic (*lasan*), minced	¾ tsp / 4 cloves
Ginger (*adrak*), minced	¾ tsp / ¾" piece

Vegetable oil	3 tbsp / 45 ml
Onion, large, finely sliced	1
Salt	¾ tsp / 3 gm
Vinegar (*sirka*)	1 tbsp / 15 ml

Method:

1. Peel off the hard outer fibre of the drumsticks.
2. Heat the oil in a pan; sauté the onion till soft. Add the ground spice paste and sauté for 1 minute.
3. Add the drumsticks. Stir well. Add ½ cup water and salt; cook covered on low heat until done.
4. Add vinegar and cook for 2 minutes more. Adjust seasoning. Serve hot.

Variations: *Use 250 gm of any vegetable especially gherkins cut lengthways or chopped cluster beans.*

Add a few peeled prawns together with vegetables like bottle gourd, aubergine, and okra. Add extra water to make a curry.

Arroz com Coco
Coconut pulao

Preparation time: 20 min.
Cooking time: 25 min.
Serves: 3-4

Ingredients:

Rice, long-grained, washed	1 cup / 200 gm
Coconut (*nariyal*), grated	2¾ cups / 200 gm
Ghee	1 tbsp / 15 gm
Onion, medium, finely sliced	1
Cloves (*laung*)	4
Cinnamon (*dalchini*), 1″ sticks	2
Green cardamoms (*choti elaichi*)	2
Turmeric (*haldi*) powder	¼ tsp
Sugar	¼ tsp
Salt	1½ tsp / 6 gm
Onion, medium, thinly sliced, fried	1
Cashew nuts (*kaju*), fried	8-10
Raisins (*kishmish*), fried	1 tbsp / 10 gm

Method:

1. Blend the coconut with 2 cups of warm water to extract 2 cups of coconut milk. Keep aside.
2. Heat the ghee in a pan; sauté the onion, cloves, cinnamon sticks, and green cardamoms for approximately 3 minutes.
3. Add the rice and stir-fry for 1 minute. Add the turmeric powder, sugar, salt, and the coconut milk. Stir well. Bring the mixture to the boil, lower heat, cover and simmer till the rice is cooked.
4. Serve garnished with fried onion, cashew nuts, and raisins.

Arroz de Camarão
Prawn pulao

Preparation time: 20 min.
Cooking time: 40 min.
Serves: 6

Ingredients:

Prawns, whole, unshelled, washed	500 gm
Rice, long-grained	2 cups / 400 gm
Ghee	4 tbsp / 60 gm
Onions, medium, finely sliced	2
Cloves (*laung*)	4
Cinnamon (*dalchini*), 1″ sticks	3
Green cardamoms (*choti elaichi*)	3
Garlic (*lasan*), minced	2 tsp / 12 cloves
Ginger (*adrak*), chopped	2 tsp / 2″ piece
Tomato, large, chopped	1
Green chillies, chopped	1-2
Turmeric (*haldi*) powder	¼ tsp
Coconut (*nariyal*) milk	1 cup / 200 ml
Salt	2 tsp / 8 gm
Sugar	½ tsp / 1½ gm

Method:

1. Remove the heads and shells of the prawns. Boil the prawns in 3 cups water for 20 minutes. Strain to extract 3 cups of stock.
2. Devein the prawns, apply a little salt; keep aside.
3. Heat the ghee in a pan; sauté the onions till lightly browned. Add the whole spices; sauté for 30 seconds. Add the garlic and ginger; sauté for a minute. Add the tomato, green chillies, and turmeric powder; stir-fry till tomatoes are pulpy. Add the prawns and stir-fry for 2 minutes till they change colour. Add rice and stir-fry for 1 minute.
4. Mix in the stock, coconut milk, salt, and sugar. Bring the mixture to the boil, lower heat and simmer, covered, till the rice is done. Serve hot.

Arroz Refogado
Chicken / lamb pulao

Preparation time: 15 min.
Cooking time: 20 min.
Serves: 4-6

Ingredients:

Rice, long-grained	2 cups / 400 gm
Vegetable oil	4 tbsp / 60 ml
Cloves (*laung*)	5
Cinnamon (*dalchini*), 1" sticks	2
Onions, medium, finely sliced	2
Garlic (*lasan*), minced	1 tsp / 6 cloves
Ginger (*adrak*), minced	1 tsp / 1" piece
Turmeric (*haldi*) powder (optional)	½ tsp / 1 gm
Tomato, large, chopped	1
Chicken / lamb stock (see p. 11)	4 cups / 800 ml
Salt	1½ tsp / 6 gm
Cooked chicken / lamb	1 cup / 200 gm

Method:

1. Heat the oil in a pan; add the cloves and cinnamon sticks and sauté for 30 seconds.

2. Add the onions and fry till soft. Add the garlic and ginger; sauté for 30 seconds. Add the turmeric powder and tomato; sauté till soft and pulpy.

3. Add the rice and stir-fry for 1 minute. Add the chicken / lamb stock and salt.

4. Add the meat and bring the mixture to the boil. Cover the pan, lower heat and simmer for 15 minutes till the rice is cooked.

5. Serve hot with chouriço (see p. 10) and lamb, chicken or pork curry.

Sanna
Steamed rice cakes

Preparation time: 12-15 hrs.
Cooking time: 30 min.
Serves: 6

Ingredients:

Parboiled rice, raw	1 cups / 200 gm
Rice, raw	½ cup / 100 gm
Coconut (*nariyal*), grated	²/₃ cup / 50 gm
Active dry yeast	¾ tsp
or	
Toddy (see p. 10)	1½ cups / 300 ml
Sugar	3-4 tbsp / 60-80 gm
Salt to taste	

Method:

1. Wash and soak the rice overnight or for at least 8 hours. Drain and grind to a fine paste with coconut and a little water or toddy, if using to a thick smooth paste.

2. If using yeast, mix 1 tsp sugar with ½ cup warm water in a bowl and sprinkle the yeast over it. Leave for a few minutes to froth.

3. In a large bowl, mix together the rice-coconut paste, sugar, salt, and yeast mixture or remaining toddy, and enough water to make a thick batter. Cover bowl and leave to rise, undisturbed, in a warm place for at least 4 hours or till batter doubles in volume.

4. Grease small steaming moulds. Pour a little batter into each mould, leaving enough room for it to rise

5. Steam for 10-15 minutes till fluffy but cooked through. *Sanna* (see p. 49 for photograph) are traditionally served with *sarapatel* (see p. 48).

Chetnim de Manga
Mango coconut chutney

Preparation time: 15 min.
Serves: 4

Accompaniments

Ingredients:

Mangoes, unripe, peeled,
  chopped   1 cup / 100 gm
Coconut (*nariyal*), grated   1¼ cups / 100 gm
Onion, small, chopped   1
Green chillies, chopped   2
Ginger (*adrak*), chopped   ½ tsp / ½" piece
Salt to taste

Method:

1. Grind all the ingredients to a coarse paste.
2. Serve with rice and curry.

*(Photograph on facing page, **centre**)*

72

Chetnim de Cilantro
Green coriander chutney

Preparation time: 15 min.
Makes: 1½ cups

Ingredients:

Coconut (*nariyal*), grated	1¼ cups / 100 gm
Green coriander (*hara dhaniya*), chopped	1½ cups / 150 gm
Green chillies, chopped	3
Garlic (*lasan*), chopped	1 tsp / 6 cloves
Cumin (*jeera*) seeds	1 tsp / 2 gm
Salt	¾ tsp / 3 gm
Granulated sugar	1 tsp / 3 gm
Lemon (*nimbu*) juice	2-3 tsp / 10-15 ml
Water	½ cup / 100 ml

Method:

1. Grind all the ingredients to a smooth paste.
2. Use as a filling with butter in sandwiches, as a topping on savoury biscuits or as a filling in *peixe recheado* (see p. 28).

*(Photograph on page 73, **top right**)*

74

Chetnim de Camarões Secos
Dried prawn chutney

Preparation time: 10 min.
Cooking time: 5 min.
Serves: 4

Ingredients:

Dried prawns (see p. 10)	1 cup / 50 gm
Kashmiri chilli powder	1 tsp / 2 gm
Turmeric (*haldi*) powder	a pinch
Onion, medium, minced	1
Garlic (*lasan*), minced	¼ tsp / 2 cloves
Tamarind (*imli*) pulp	2 tsp
Coconut (*nariyal*), grated	5 tbsp / 20 gm
Salt to taste	

Method:

1. Clean the prawns, pinch off the top part of the head, tip of the tail and legs. Dry roast in a frying pan till crisp.
2. Mix the rest of the ingredients in a bowl and crumble the prawns into the mixture. Stir to mix.
3. Alternatively, sauté the onion and garlic in a little oil for a few minutes, then grind with the rest of the ingredients to a coarse paste.
4. Serve as an accompaniment to rice and curry.

*(Photograph on page 73, **top left**)*

Balchão de Camarão
Spicy prawn pickle

Preparation time: 30 min.
Cooking time: 20 min.
Makes: 1 bottle

Ingredients:

Prawns, small, shelled, deveined	1¼ cups / 250 gm

Grind to a smooth paste with 6 tbsp vinegar:

Kashmiri chillies (*sookhi lal mirch*)	10-12
Cumin (*jeera*) seeds	1 tsp / 2 gm
Mustard seeds (*rai*), optional	½ tsp / 1 gm
Black peppercorns (*sabut kali mirch*)	½ tsp / 1 gm
Turmeric (*haldi*) powder	½ tsp / 1 gm
Garlic (*lasan*), chopped	3 tsp / 18 cloves
Ginger (*adrak*), chopped	2 tsp / 2″ piece

Vegetable oil	1 cup / 200 ml
Onions, medium, chopped	2
Curry leaves (*kadhi patta*)	8-10
Vinegar (*sirka*)	6 tbsp / 90 ml
Green chillies, slit	2
Salt to taste	
Sugar	2 tsp / 6 gm

Method:

1. Heat the oil in a pan; sauté the onions till soft and golden. Add the curry leaves and the ground paste; sauté for 3 minutes, stirring constantly.
2. Add the prawns and stir-fry for a few minutes.
3. Add the vinegar, green chillies, salt, and sugar. Cook uncovered for 10 minutes Adjust seasoning.
4. Remove from heat. Bottle when cool. Serve with rice and curry. Or use as a filling in *paparis recheados* (see p. 16) and *pasteis de camarão* (see p. 19).

Manguinhas Salgadas (Chepnim)

Mangoes in brine

Ingredients:

Green mangoes, unripe, small, tender	25
Coarse sea salt	2 cups
Kashmiri chillies (*sookhi lal mirch*)	6-8
Asafoetida (*hing*) powder	½ tsp / 2½ gm

Method:

1. Choose mangoes with soft seeds. Wash and wipe them dry. Keep whole.

2. Take a large glass / porcelain / enamel basin. Sprinkle some salt at the bottom. Layer the mangoes, chillies, and asafoetida, ending with a layer of salt. Place a small plate on the mangoes and rest a heavy-weight on it so that the mangoes get pressed down. Cover the basin with a muslin cloth. Leave to salt for 3 days.

3. Uncover the basin and turn the mangoes over. Sprinkle a little more salt. Replace the weight and cover. Repeat the process after 3 days. There should be quite a lot of liquid.

4. Transfer the mangoes with the brine into a glass jar, ensuring that they are completely submerged in the brine. Leave to mature for at least 2 weeks. The mangoes will have a wrinkled appearance.

5. When ready, remove as many mangoes as required with a dry, slotted spoon, ensuring that the remaining mangoes are covered with the brine. Cut in long slices. Serve with rice and curry.

Chetnim Doce de Manga
Sweet mango chutney

Preparation time: 20 min.
Cooking time: 20 min.
Makes: 1 bottle

Ingredients:

Mangoes, half-riped, skinned, grated coarsely	2½ cups / 500 gm
Granulated sugar	1¼ cups / 200 gm
Vinegar (*sirka*)	½ cup / 100 ml
Ginger (*adrak*), minced	2 tsp / 2″ piece
Garlic (*lasan*), minced	2 tsp / 12 cloves
Kashmiri chilli powder	1½-2 tsp / 3-4 gm
Salt	2 tsp / 8 gm
Raisins (*kishmish*)	2 tbsp / 25 gm

Method:

1. In a pan, cook the mangoes and the sugar on low heat till the sugar melts.
2. Add the rest of the ingredients, except the raisins, and cook till the mixture is thick. Add the raisins and cook for 2 more minutes. Adjust seasoning.
3. Remove from heat and cool. Bottle when cold. Allow to mature for a week.

(*Photograph on page 79*, **top**: *Manguinhas Salgadas;* **bottom left:** *Chetnim Doce de Manga;* **bottom right:** *Achar de Tendlim*)

Achar de Tendlim
Gherkin pickle

Preparation time: 2½ hrs.
Makes: 1 bottle

Ingredients:

Gherkins (*tindli*), washed, wiped dry	500 gm
Salt	3 tsp / 12 gm

Grind to a smooth paste with 6 tbsp vinegar:

Kashmiri chillies (*sookhi lal mirch*)	10-12
Mustard seeds (*rai*)	½ tsp / 1 gm
Cumin (*jeera*) seeds	½ tsp / 1 gm
Turmeric (*haldi*) powder	½ tsp / 1 gm
Garlic (*lasan*), minced	4 tsp / 20-25 cloves
Ginger (*adrak*), minced	2 tsp / 2" piece
Vegetable oil	1 cup / 200 ml
Curry leaves (*kadhi patta*)	10-12
Vinegar (*sirka*)	7 tbsp / 105 ml
Sugar	3-4 tbsp / 60-80 gm
Green chillies, slit	2

Method:

1. Cut each gherkin lengthways into 6 pieces. Apply 3 tsp salt and keep aside for at least 2 hours. Squeeze out the excess water and spread out on kitchen towels to dry for a while.
2. Heat the oil in a pan; sauté the curry leaves for a few seconds. Add the spice paste and fry well for 3 minutes. Add the gherkins and fry lightly.
3. Add the vinegar, sugar, and green chillies. Mix well and cook on moderate heat for 10-15 minutes, stirring from time to time, till the gherkins are cooked, but still retain some of their crispness.
4. Adjust seasoning. Remove from heat and cool. Bottle when cold.

Bebinca
Layered dessert

Preparation time: 30 min.
Cooking time: 1½ hrs.
Serves: 6-8

Ingredients:

Coconut (*nariyal*), grated	2⅓ cups / 200 gm
Granulated sugar	2⅔ cups / 400 gm
Egg yolks, beaten lightly	10
Refined flour (*maida*)	1 cup / 100 gm
Salt	½ tsp / 2 gm
Nutmeg / green cardamom	
(*jaiphal* / *choti elaichi*) powder	¼ tsp
Ghee, melted	¾ cup / 125 gm

Method:

1. Preheat the oven to 350°F / 180°C.
2. Extract 1 cup of thick coconut milk by grinding the coconut with 1 cup warm water. Grind the coconut again with 1 cup warm water and extract 1 cup of thin coconut milk.
3. Dissolve the sugar in the thin coconut milk in a pan over low heat. Keep aside to cool. Mix in the egg yolks, a little at a time. Stir in the thick coconut milk. Gradually add the remaining ingredients except ghee. Mix till the batter is smooth. Strain.
4. Pour 3 tbsp ghee into a 7"-round, deep baking tin. Then pour 1 cup batter over the ghee and bake for 10 minutes till set and the top is golden. Pour 1 tbsp ghee over the baked layer and then ¾ cup batter, bake or grill again till golden. Continue till all the batter is used up. There should be 7 layers.
5. When cool turn the *bebinca* out on to a plate. Leave to set for at least 12 hours before slicing.

Ale Bele
Coconut crêpes

Preparation time: 15 min.
Cooking time: 15 min.
Makes: 12

Ingredients:

For the crêpes:

Refined flour (*maida*)	1¼ cups / 125 gm
Baking powder	a pinch
Salt	¼ tsp / 1 gm
Egg	1
Granulated sugar	1 tbsp / 20 gm
Milk / half milk and half water	1 cup + 3 tbsp / 240 ml

For the filling:

Sugar / grated jaggery (*gur*), dissolved in 1 tbsp water over low heat	3 tbsp / 60 gm
Coconut (*nariyal*), grated	2 cups / 150 gm
Ghee for frying	

Method:

1. Mix all the dry ingredients together in a bowl.
2. Beat the egg with the sugar till foamy. Mix in the milk / milk and water. Pour this gradually into the flour mixture to prevent lumps from forming. Beat well for 1 minute. Leave to stand for 15 minutes.
3. Grease and heat a 6″ frying pan lightly with ghee; pour 2 tbsp batter into it, tilting to coat the base thinly. Cook covered for a minute. Remove and repeat till all the batter is used up.
4. **For the filling**, in a pan, add the sugar / jaggery syrup and coconut; cook for a few seconds. Remove from heat and cool.
5. Place a little filling on each pancake and roll tightly.
6. Serve on a dish and sprinkle with grated coconut.

Rose de Coco
Fried waffles

Preparation time: 20 min.
Cooking time: 20 min.
Makes: 18 waffles

Ingredients:

Refined flour (*maida*)	1¾ cups / 175 gm
Salt	¼ tsp / 1 gm
Eggs	2
Castor sugar	3 tbsp / 60 gm
Milk / coconut milk	1½ cups / 300 ml
Vanilla essence	½ tsp / 2½ ml
Vegetable oil for deep-frying	

Method:

1. Sift the flour and salt together.
2. Beat the eggs with the sugar till thick and foamy. Stir in the milk and vanilla essence and mix well.
3. Add the egg mixture to the flour, gradually, stirring well to make a smooth, thin batter. Leave the batter to rest for 15 minutes.
4. Heat the oil well. Rest the waffle iron (mould) in the hot oil for 2 minutes to heat. Remove and dip immediately into the batter, making sure that the batter coats only the bottom and the sides of the mould and does not go over the top. Transfer immediately to the hot oil. Hold the iron in the oil till the waffle is golden brown and loosens easily. Remove and drain on a plate lined with paper towels. Continue till all the batter is over, heating the mould for a few seconds in the oil before dipping into the batter each time.
5. Cool and store in an airtight container.

Perada

Guava cheese

Preparation time: 30 min.
Cooking time: 40 min.
Makes: 40-50 pieces

Ingredients:

Guavas, medium, peeled	6
Granulated sugar as required	
Lemon (*nimbu*) juice	1-2 tsp / 5-10 ml
Butter (optional)	1 tsp
Red food colour, optional	few drops

Method:

1. Cut the guavas in half and scoop out the seeds. Cook the seeds with ¼ cup water for a few minutes. Strain through a sieve. Reserve the liquid and discard the seeds.

2. Chop the guavas and cook in a pan with 1 cup water and the reserved liquid till soft and pulpy.

3. Cool for a while and process in a blender till smooth. Weigh the pulp.

4. Return the pulp to the pan with the sugar (which should be half the weight of the guava pulp) and cook, stirring continuously, till the mixture begins to leave the sides of the pan and is of soft-ball consistency. Add the lemon juice, butter, and red food colour, if using. Stir well; remove from heat.

5. Pour the mixture on to a greased board or plate and spread evenly with the back of a greased spoon. Cut into diamond shapes when cold.

Letria
Coconut and bread sweet

Preparation time: 20 min.
Cooking time: 30 min.
Serves: 4-6

Ingredients:

Granulated sugar	1⅓ cups / 200 gm
Water	4 tbsp / 60 ml
Egg yolks, optional	2
Coconut (*nariyal*), white part only, grated	2 cups / 200 gm
Fresh bread cubes, crust removed	1 cup / 50 gm
Raisins (*kishmish*), washed	1 tbsp / 10 gm
Cashew nuts (*kaju*) / almonds (*badam*), blanched, chopped	1 tbsp / 15 gm
Butter / ghee	1 tsp / 5 gm

Method:

1. Dissolve the sugar in the water in a pan over moderate heat.
2. If using, beat the egg yolks well. Pour into an icing bag with a very fine nozzle. Drizzle the egg yolk into the hot sugar syrup in a lacy pattern. When set, lift out with a slotted spoon and leave to cool.
3. Add the coconut and bread to the remaining sugar syrup and cook till it comes together and the moisture is absorbed (approximately 5-7 minutes). Do not let the mixture get too dry.
4. Add the dried fruits and butter / ghee; mix well.
5. Pour on to a greased plate and leave to set. Gently arrange the cooked egg yolk on top, if desired.

Bolo de Coco
Coconut and semolina cake

Preparation time: 15 min.
Cooking time: 40 min.
Serves: 6

Ingredients:

Semolina (*suji*)	1¼ cups / 175 gm
Granulated sugar	1⅓ cups / 200 gm
Water	4 tbsp / 60 ml
Coconut (*nariyal*), grated	2 cups / 150 gm
Butter	4 tbsp / 60 gm
Vanilla essence	½ tsp
Baking powder	1 tsp / 6 gm
Eggs, separated	3

Method:

1. Preheat the oven to 350°F / 180°C .
2. In a pan, dissolve the sugar in water over low heat. Add the coconut and cook for 2 minutes. Add butter, semolina, and vanilla essence; mix well. Remove from heat and keep aside to cool.
3. Mix in the baking powder to the cooled mixture.
4. Beat the egg yolks till thick and foamy and stir into the mixture. Beat the egg whites till stiff and gently fold into the mixture.
5. Pour into a greased, 9"-round cake tin and bake for 25-30 minutes until well-risen and golden.
6. Let it cool in the tin for 10 minutes. Turn out on to a wire rack and cool.

Note: *The traditional method of making this cake is to mix the ingredients and keep it overnight to rise, omitting the use of baking powder.*

Suggested Menus

Non-vegetarian

Galinha Cafreal (*Spicy fried / grilled chicken*) 52

Caril de Camarão (*Prawn curry*) 40

Peixe Recheado (*Fish stuffed with red spice paste*)28

or

Vegetarian

Beringelas Picantes (*Spicy aubergine*) 58

Melgor / Alsande (*Black-eyed bean curry*) 63

Accompaniments

Steamed Rice

Achar de Tendlim (*Gherkin pickle*) 81

Dessert

Letria (*Coconut and bread sweet*) 90

Non-vegetarian

Bombil Frito (*Fried fresh Bombay duck*) 37

Caril de Almondegas de Carne (*Meat ball curry*)46

Vindalho de Carne de Porco
(*Pork curry flavoured with garlic and vinegar*) 51

or

Vegetarian

Fugad de Repolho (*Steamed cabbage*) 60

Xengo Temperado (*Curried drumsticks*) 64

Accompaniments

Arroz com Coco (*Coconut pulao*) 66

Chetnim de Manga (*Mango coconut chutney*) 72

Dessert

Bebinca (*Layered dessert*) 82

Glossary of Cooking Terms

Batter — A mixture of flour, liquid and sometimes other ingredients, of a thin or thick consistency.

Blend — To mix together thoroughly two or more ingredients.

Coat — To cover food that is to be fried with flour, egg and breadcrumbs or batter.

Fry — To cook in hot fat or oil. In the case of shallow frying only a small quantity of fat is used in a shallow pan. The food must be turned halfway through to cook both sides. In the case of deep-frying, sufficient fat is used to cover the food completely.

Marinade — A seasoned mixture of oil, vinegar, lemon juice, and so forth, in which meat, poultry or fish is left for some time to soften and add flavour to it.

Rub in — To incorporate the fat into flour using the fingertips.

Sauté — To cook in an open pan in hot, shallow fat, tossing the food to prevent it from sticking.

Simmer — To boil gently on low heat.

Stir-fry — Fry rapidly while stirring and tossing.

Index

ISBN: 978-81-7436-195-0

Third impression 2007
© **Roli & Janssen BV**
Published in India by
Roli Books in arrangement with
Roli & Janssen
M-75 Greater Kailash II (Market)
New Delhi 110 048, India
Ph: (011) 29212271, 29212782, 29210886
Fax: (011) 29217185, E-mail: roli@vsnl.com
Website: rolibooks.com

Photographs: Dheeraj Paul

Printed and bound in Singapore